The Arctic Vortex

Showdown at the Top of the World

By

MILTON ROTHBARD

Printed in the United States of America.

Disclaimer

This is a work of fiction. Names, characters, organizations, governments, corporations, locations, and incidents are either products of the author's imagination or are used fictitiously. Any resemblance to actual persons, living or dead, or to actual events, locales, or institutions is purely coincidental.

The geopolitical scenarios, economic analyses, and strategic interpretations presented in this book are fictionalized for narrative purposes. While the story may reference real countries, regions, or global issues, these elements are used solely to create an immersive and educational fictional narrative. Nothing in this book should be interpreted as factual reporting, political prediction, or authoritative analysis.

The depictions of national policies, military capabilities, economic conditions, and international relations are imaginative constructs and do not represent the official positions, actions, or intentions of any government, agency, or organization.

This book does not provide legal, financial, political, or professional advice. Readers should exercise their own judgment and consult qualified professionals for guidance on real-world matters.

Milton Rothbard

“Every fiction carries a shard of truth,
for imagination is merely reality wearing a more beautiful disguise.”

Milton Rothbard

PROLOGUE

The Arctic Circle — 78° North
Midwinter

The wind moved first.

A low, ancient moan rolled across the ice shelf, as if the Earth itself were exhaling after holding its breath for a thousand years. The sky above was a bruised violet, the kind of color that existed only in places where the sun forgot to rise. The horizon was a blade of silver, sharp enough to cut the world in half.

And in that vast, frozen silence, something shifted.

Not loudly. Not violently.
But with the quiet authority of a giant turning in its sleep.

Sensors buried deep beneath the ice began to tremble. Satellites orbiting far above adjusted their trajectories by fractions of a degree. Submarines—silent, patient, predatory—felt the pressure change in their steel bones.

The Arctic Vortex had stirred.
For centuries, the top of the world had been a place of myth and mystery, a blank space on maps where explorers vanished and compasses lied. But now, in the age of satellites and supercomputers, the Arctic was no longer a frontier.

It was a prize.

A reservoir of minerals older than empires.

A corridor of shipping lanes faster than any canal.
A vault of energy buried beneath a kingdom of ice.
A stage where nations measured their strength without firing a shot.

And tonight, the stage was shifting.

A single crack echoed across the frozen plain—thin, delicate, almost polite. But beneath it, miles below the surface, tectonic plates whispered secrets to one another. The vortex tightened, its spiraling winds pulling cold air southward like a warning.

In a research station perched on the edge of the world, a lone scientist pressed her gloved hand against the window. She watched the ice tremble under the weight of forces no human could command. Her breath fogged the glass, a small, fragile cloud in a land ruled by giants.
She whispered to herself, not out of fear, but reverence.

"Something's coming."

Not a war.
Not an invasion.
Something quieter.
Something colder.
A contest of presence, pressure, and power—fought in shadows, in silence, in the spaces between nations.

Far away, in capitals lit by warm electric light, leaders would soon feel the shift. Economists would sense it in the markets. Admirals would see it in the currents. Corporations would smell opportunity. Intelligence agencies would hear whispers.

But here, at the top of the world, the truth arrived first.

The Arctic was awakening.

And the world—unprepared, distracted, divided—was about to learn that the most dangerous battles are the ones fought without bullets...
and the most powerful forces are the ones no one sees.

CHAPTER I — THE FIRST SIGNAL

Svalbard Global Observatory
03:14 UTC

The alarm didn't scream.
It whispered.

A soft, pulsing tone—barely louder than a heartbeat—echoed through the dimly lit control room. Dr. Elena Markov lifted her head from a stack of satellite telemetry, her eyes narrowing. The Arctic didn't tolerate noise. Anything loud was either a mistake or a disaster.

She tapped the console.
The whispering alarm grew into a slow, rhythmic pulse.

Pressure anomaly.
Upper-atmospheric shear.
Magnetic drift.

Three readings, all rising in perfect, unnatural harmony.

Elena felt the familiar tightening in her chest. She had seen anomalies before—solar flares, geomagnetic storms, even the occasional Russian satellite test—but this was different. This was coordinated. Synchronized. Intentional.

The Arctic Vortex was shifting again.

She leaned closer to the screen. The data streams danced like nervous handwriting. The vortex's core had contracted by 0.7

percent in the last hour—an almost impossible rate. And yet, the numbers didn't lie.

Something was pulling the atmosphere tighter.

Something big.

She reached for her radio, hesitated, then pulled her hand back. No. Not yet. Not without confirmation.

Instead, she opened the encrypted channel to the observatory's deep-ice sensors. A map of the Arctic seabed flickered to life—dark blues, pale greens, and a single, pulsing red dot.

A submarine.
Moving slowly.
Too slowly.

Elena frowned. Submarines didn't crawl like that unless they were mapping something... or hiding.

She zoomed in.
The signature was faint, masked, almost elegant in its deception.

Not American.
Not Russian.
Not any nation she recognized.

Her breath caught.

A new player.

The Arctic had always been a chessboard, but tonight, someone had moved a piece she didn't know existed.

She stood, crossed the room, and pressed her palm against the reinforced glass window. Outside, the polar night stretched endlessly, a cathedral of ice and shadow. The wind howled softly, as if trying to warn her.

Behind her, the console beeped again—this time louder.

The vortex had tightened another 0.3 percent.

Elena whispered to the empty room, "This isn't natural."

And she was right.

Thousands of kilometers away, in Washington, Moscow, Beijing, Ottawa, and Oslo, encrypted intelligence channels were lighting up with the same anomaly. Admirals were waking from sleep. Economists were checking commodity futures. Energy ministers were calling emergency meetings.

But none of them knew what Elena knew:

The Arctic wasn't reacting.
It was responding.

To what, she didn't yet understand.
But she felt it—deep in her bones, the way her father once felt storms before they formed.

A shift in the world.
A tightening of something invisible.
A silent flex of power at the top of the Earth.

She turned back to the console, her voice steady now.

"Log event," she said. "Codename: First Signal."

The computer complied.

Outside, the wind rose, carrying with it the first hint of a truth the world had forgotten:

The Arctic keeps its secrets...
until it decides not to.

"The world rarely notices the first tremor.
It only remembers the moment everything shifts."
— Arvid Lehtinen, Finnish Polar Meteorologist (1978)

CHAPTER II — THE QUIET PANIC

Washington, D.C. Strategic Intelligence Center
04:02 EST

The room was too quiet.

Not the peaceful kind of quiet, but the kind that settles over a place when everyone inside is pretending they're not afraid. Screens glowed in cold blues and greens, casting long shadows across the faces of analysts who had been awake far too long.

At the center of the room stood Director Samuel Harrington, a man carved from the same granite as the institutions he served. His hair was silver, his posture rigid, his eyes sharp enough to cut through lies and data alike.

He stared at the satellite feed on the main screen.

A swirling mass of atmospheric distortion hovered over the Arctic Circle—dense, tight, unnatural. The vortex had contracted again. Not by much. But enough.

Enough to matter.
Enough to worry him.
"Run it again," Harrington said.

The analyst beside him swallowed hard. "Sir, this is the fifth pass. The readings are consistent."

"Run it again."

The analyst obeyed.

The vortex tightened by another fraction of a percent.

Harrington exhaled slowly. “That’s not weather.”

“No, sir,” the analyst whispered. “It isn’t.”

A second screen flickered to life—this one showing a faint sonar trace moving beneath the ice. The same trace Elena Markov had seen hours earlier. The same trace that had now been detected by three separate listening posts.

A submarine.
Slow.
Silent.
Masking its signature with a sophistication no known navy possessed.

Harrington leaned closer. “Origin?”

“Unknown, sir.”

“Classification?”

“Unknown.”

“Intent?”

The analyst hesitated. “Also unknown.”

Harrington straightened. “So we know nothing.”

“Not nothing,” said a voice behind him.

Dr. Aisha Rahmani stepped forward, her dark hair tied back, her expression calm but alert. She was the agency’s top atmospheric physicist, a woman whose mind moved faster than most computers.
She pointed at the vortex data. “This isn’t a natural contraction. It’s too symmetrical. Too controlled.”

“Controlled by what?” Harrington asked.

“Not what,” she said softly. “Who.”

The room fell silent.

Aisha continued, “Someone is manipulating the upper-atmospheric pressure gradients. Not enough to cause a storm. Just enough to… signal.”

“Signal what?”

“That they can.”

Harrington felt a chill crawl up his spine. Power wasn’t always shown through force. Sometimes it was shown through precision—through the ability to touch the world without leaving fingerprints.

“And the submarine?” he asked.

Aisha nodded. “Part of the same message.”

Harrington turned back to the screens. The vortex pulsed like a heartbeat. The submarine trace glided like a shadow.

A show of force.
Silent.
Calculated.
Deliberate.

He tapped the table. "Who else knows?"

"Only us," Aisha said. "For now."

"Good. Keep it that way."

He walked toward the exit, his footsteps echoing in the sterile room. Before he reached the door, he paused.

"Doctor," he said without turning, "if someone is doing this... what do they want?"

Aisha looked at the vortex, her voice barely above a whisper. "Attention."
"Influence is the art of moving the world without letting the world see your hand."
— Lucía Valverde, Argentine Diplomat (1994)

CHAPTER III — THE SHADOW IN THE ICE

Moscow Ministry of Natural Resources
12:47 MSK

The minister's office was warm, almost uncomfortably so. Heavy curtains blocked the winter light, and the air smelled faintly of old leather and stronger tea. Minister Viktor Sokolov sat behind a polished walnut desk, his fingers drumming a slow, deliberate rhythm.

He wasn't a man easily rattled.
But today, something was wrong.

Across from him, Colonel Irina Volkov stood at attention, her uniform immaculate, her expression carved from stone. She placed a sealed folder on the desk.

"Satellite Division confirms it," she said. "The vortex is contracting unnaturally."

Sokolov didn't open the folder. He didn't need to. He had already seen the preliminary data. He had spent the last six hours staring at it, trying to convince himself it was a glitch.

It wasn't.
"And the submarine?" he asked.

Irina hesitated. "Not ours. Not theirs. Not anyone's."

Sokolov leaned back, exhaling slowly. "Impossible."

"Sir," she said, "the Arctic does not care what we think is possible."

He finally opened the folder. Inside were high-resolution images of the vortex, sonar traces, and a classified report from the Northern Fleet. The submarine's movement was precise, almost surgical. It moved like a creature that knew the ice better than the nations circling it.

Sokolov closed the folder.

"Who else knows?" he asked.

"Washington. Beijing. Oslo. Ottawa. And the Svalbard Observatory."

He nodded. "So the whole world."

Irina allowed herself the faintest smirk. "The part of the world that matters."

Sokolov stood and walked to the window. Snow fell in slow spirals, soft and silent. Moscow looked peaceful, but he knew better. Peace was a mask. Underneath it, nations sharpened their ambitions like knives.

"Colonel," he said, "what do you think this is?"

Irina didn't answer immediately. She chose her words with the precision of a surgeon.

"A demonstration."

"Of what?"

"Capability."

Sokolov turned. "Whose capability?"

Irina met his gaze. "Someone who wants us to know they're there… but not who they are."

A chill ran through him. Not from fear — from recognition.
This was strategy.
This was theater.
This was a message written in wind and ice.

He walked back to his desk and tapped the folder.

"Prepare a briefing for the President," he said. "And send a discreet inquiry to our friends in Murmansk. I want to know if any of our deep-sea drones have detected unusual mineral activity."

Irina raised an eyebrow. "Minerals, sir?"

Sokolov nodded. "If someone is manipulating the vortex, they're not doing it for sport. They're doing it for resources."

Irina understood immediately.
Rare earths.
Methane hydrates.
Sub-glacial metals untouched since the Pleistocene.

The Arctic wasn't just a frontier.
It was a vault.

And someone had found the key.

As Irina turned to leave, Sokolov added, "Colonel… keep this quiet. The last thing we need is panic."

Irina paused at the door. "Panic is loud, Minister. This… this will be silent."

She left.

Sokolov sat alone, staring at the folder.
The vortex pulsed on the screen like a living thing.
The submarine trace glided like a ghost.

He whispered to himself, "Who are you?"

Outside, the snow continued to fall — soft, steady, indifferent — as if the city had no idea that far to the north, the world's balance was beginning to tilt.

"Power rarely announces itself.
It arrives quietly, and only the wise notice."
— Nikolai Arsenyev, Russian Arctic Historian (1962)

CHAPTER IV — THE MAP NO ONE ADMITS EXISTS

Beijing, Institute for Polar Strategy
09:11 CST

Dr. Jianyu Zhao did not like being summoned.

He especially did not like being summoned without explanation, without agenda, and without the usual diplomatic pleasantries that softened the edges of Beijing's bureaucracy. But when the call came at dawn, he dressed, shaved, and walked through the marble corridors of the Institute with the calm precision of a man who understood that irritation was a luxury.

He entered the conference room.

Three people were already there.

None of them smiled.

At the head of the table sat Vice-Minister Liang, a man whose expression rarely changed and whose silence carried more weight than most speeches. To his left, Admiral Chen of the Northern Fleet. To his right, Professor Mei Lin, the Institute's chief economist and the only person in the building who could intimidate Jianyu intellectually.

Liang gestured to the empty chair.

"Sit."

Jianyu obeyed.

The lights dimmed. A screen descended.
Satellite imagery filled the room — swirling winds, pressure gradients, and the unmistakable tightening of the Arctic Vortex.

Jianyu's pulse quickened.

"You've seen this?" Liang asked.

"Yes," Jianyu replied. "But not at this resolution."

Admiral Chen leaned forward. "Then you understand the implications."

Jianyu nodded slowly. "Someone is manipulating the upper atmosphere."

Professor Mei Lin tapped her pen. "And someone is moving beneath the ice."

The screen shifted to sonar data — the same ghostly submarine trace that had unsettled Washington and Moscow.

Jianyu frowned. "Not Russian. Not American. Not ours."

"Correct," Admiral Chen said. "Which leaves us with a problem."

Liang folded his hands. "Dr. Zhao, you are our foremost expert on Arctic geopolitics. Tell us what we are looking at."

Jianyu inhaled deeply.

"A demonstration," he said. "A controlled, deliberate display of capability. Someone is showing they can influence the Arctic without being detected."

"And why would they do that?" Mei Lin asked.

Jianyu turned to her. "Because the Arctic is the last unclaimed balance sheet on Earth."

Mei Lin's eyes glimmered. "Go on."

"The minerals beneath the ice," Jianyu said. "The methane hydrates. The rare earth deposits. The shipping lanes that will cut transit times in half. Whoever controls the Arctic controls the next century of global trade."

Admiral Chen nodded. "And someone is telling us they intend to be first."

Liang tapped the table. "We need to know who."

Jianyu hesitated. "There is one possibility."

The room stilled.

"Not a nation," he said. "A consortium."

Mei Lin raised an eyebrow. "Private?"

"Private," Jianyu confirmed. "Well-funded. Well-equipped. Unbound by treaties. Unrestricted by borders."

Admiral Chen's jaw tightened. "A rogue actor."

"No," Jianyu said softly. "A strategic actor. One who understands that the Arctic is not a battlefield... but a marketplace."

Liang stood. "Find them."

Jianyu blinked. "Sir?"

"Find them," Liang repeated. "Before Washington does. Before Moscow does. Before they make their next move."

Jianyu swallowed. "And if they are already ahead?"

Liang's voice was calm, almost gentle.

"Then we catch up."

The meeting ended.
The lights brightened.
The screen retracted.

But Jianyu remained seated, staring at the empty table.

A consortium.
A private force.
A shadow with enough money, technology, and ambition to bend the Arctic to its will.
He whispered to himself, "What are you trying to build?"

Outside, Beijing hummed with life — traffic, voices, commerce — unaware that far to the north, beneath a sky that never saw daylight, a new kind of power was awakening.

Not national.
Not military.
Not ideological.

Economic.
Strategic.
Invisible.

And it had just made its first move.

"The greatest shifts in power begin not with armies, but with ambitions no one sees."
— Sofia Brandt, Swedish Geoeconomist (2003)

CHAPTER V — THE COUNCIL OF QUIET VOICES

Oslo, Arctic Council Secretariat
15:22 CET

The conference room was built for diplomacy, not urgency.
Soft lighting.
Warm wood.
A panoramic window overlooking the Oslofjord, where the water moved with the slow confidence of a nation that had mastered calm.

But today, calm was a lie.

Ambassador Ingrid Solberg stood at the head of the oval table, her posture straight, her expression composed, her mind racing. She had spent her career navigating the fragile balance of Arctic cooperation — treaties, environmental accords, resource-sharing agreements — all built on the assumption that the region would remain predictable.

Predictable was gone.

Around the table sat representatives from Canada, Denmark, Finland, Iceland, Sweden, and the United States. Russia's chair remained empty — a silent reminder of tensions that had never fully thawed.

Ingrid tapped the folder in front of her.

"Ladies and gentlemen," she began, "we have a situation."

The room shifted. Not dramatically. Just enough.

She pressed a button. The screen behind her lit up with the same images that had haunted Washington, Moscow, and Beijing: the contracting vortex, the atmospheric distortion, the ghostly submarine trace.

A murmur rippled through the room.

Dr. Henrik Dahl, Norway's leading climatologist, leaned forward. "This contraction is not meteorological. It's engineered."

The Canadian delegate frowned. "Engineered by whom?"

Henrik shook his head. "That's the problem. No known state has this capability."
The American representative cleared his throat. "We're not ruling out state actors."

Ingrid shot him a look. "You're not ruling out anything."

He didn't deny it.

The Finnish delegate adjusted her glasses. "If this is a demonstration of power, why show it to us?"

Henrik answered before Ingrid could. "Because the Arctic Council is the only body that can legitimize new claims. Whoever is doing this wants us to know they exist."

The room fell silent.

Ingrid stepped closer to the screen. "This is not an attack. Not a provocation. It's a message."

The Icelandic representative raised an eyebrow. "What kind of message?"

Ingrid exhaled slowly. "A warning shot without the shot."

Henrik nodded. "A show of force."

The American delegate leaned back. "Or a show of ownership."

That word hung in the air like frost.

Ownership.

The Arctic had always been a place of contested dreams — resources, shipping lanes, sovereignty. But no one had ever dared to claim it outright. Not openly. Not boldly.

Until now.

Ingrid closed the folder. "We need to coordinate. Quietly. No press. No leaks. No panic."

The Swedish representative asked, "And what do we tell our governments?"

Ingrid looked out the window. Snow had begun to fall — soft, delicate, indifferent.

"Tell them," she said, "that the Arctic is changing. And that someone is changing it faster than we can understand."

Henrik added, "And tell them this: the first move has already been made."

The room absorbed his words like a sponge absorbing cold water.

Ingrid straightened. "We reconvene in forty-eight hours. Bring your best analysts. Bring your best minds. And bring the assumption that we are already behind."

The delegates stood, gathering their papers, their coats, their fears.

As they filed out, Henrik approached Ingrid.

"You didn't tell them everything," he said quietly.

"No," she replied.

"Why?"

"Because the truth is worse."

Henrik swallowed. "You think this is coordinated."

"I think," Ingrid whispered, "that someone has been preparing for this moment for a very long time."

Outside, the snow thickened, falling in slow spirals — the same spirals forming far to the north, where the vortex tightened like a fist.

The world was beginning to listen.
But the Arctic had been speaking for months.

"The most dangerous power is the one that moves before anyone realizes a game has begun."
— Elias Korhonen, Finnish Strategic Analyst (1988)

CHAPTER VI — THE CONSORTIUM IN THE DARK

Zurich, Helix International Holdings
19:03 CET

The elevator rose without a sound, gliding upward like a secret being carried toward the light.
Dr. Adrian Keller stepped out onto the top floor, where the air felt different — thinner, colder, more deliberate. The boardroom ahead was a cathedral of glass and steel, suspended above the Zurich skyline like a throne room for ghosts.

Inside, six figures sat around a long obsidian table.
No names.
No introductions.
No need.

These were the people who moved the world without ever appearing in it.

Adrian took his seat. The door sealed behind him with a soft hiss.

A woman with silver hair and eyes like sharpened frost spoke first.
"Begin."

Adrian tapped his tablet. The lights dimmed. A holographic projection rose from the center of the table — swirling winds, atmospheric distortions, and the unmistakable tightening of the Arctic Vortex.

The same images that had rattled governments.

Here, they elicited something else entirely.

Interest.
Calculation.
Satisfaction.

A man in a charcoal suit leaned forward. “The vortex contraction is accelerating.”

“As predicted,” Adrian replied.

“And the submarine?” another asked.

“Still undetected in origin. But very much detected in presence.”
A faint smile touched the silver-haired woman’s lips. “Good. Let them wonder.”

Adrian swiped again. The hologram shifted to a map of the Arctic — glowing points marking strategic locations beneath the ice.

“These are the next sites,” he said. “Deep-ice fields. Pressure corridors. Thermal anomalies.”

A murmur rippled through the room.

“Perfect,” someone whispered.

The woman raised a hand. Silence returned instantly.

“Ladies and gentlemen,” she said, “the world believes it is witnessing a natural event. A meteorological curiosity. A scientific puzzle.”

She leaned back, her voice soft but razor-sharp.

“They have no idea they are watching us.”

Adrian felt the familiar chill — not fear, but awe.
This was power without borders.
Ambition without ideology.
Strategy without hesitation.

The woman continued, “Governments will posture. Agencies will panic. Committees will meet. But none of them can move as quickly as we can.”

She tapped the table lightly.

“The Arctic is shifting. And we are the ones shifting it.”

The room absorbed her words like scripture.

Adrian closed the projection. The lights brightened. The meeting dissolved into quiet, purposeful motion.

But as he walked toward the elevator, he paused at the window.
Snow drifted over Zurich — gentle, harmless, almost pretty.

Nothing like the snow far to the north.

There, the ice was trembling.

There, the vortex was tightening.
There, the world was being rewritten.

And the consortium — unseen, unknown, unchallenged — was holding the pen.

"True power is not the ability to strike.
It is the ability to shape the battlefield before anyone arrives."
— René Falk, Swiss Strategic Theorist (1999)

CHAPTER VII — THE WHISPER BENEATH THE ICE

Svalbard Global Observatory
22:19 UTC

The night was absolute.

Not the soft darkness of cities, but the ancient, crushing kind that swallowed sound and memory. The wind scraped against the metal siding of the observatory like a warning written in cold.

Dr. Elena Markov stood alone in the monitoring room, her hands wrapped around a mug of coffee gone cold hours ago. She hadn't slept. She couldn't. The data wouldn't let her.

The vortex contraction had accelerated again.

Not dramatically.
Not violently.
But with the same quiet precision she had seen in the submarine's movements.

A pattern.
A rhythm.
A pulse.

She stared at the screen, watching the atmospheric pressure lines tighten like a noose.

Behind her, the door opened with a soft click.

"Still here?" a voice asked.

Elena didn't turn. "Still pretending this is natural?"

Henrik Dahl stepped inside, rubbing his eyes. He looked exhausted — the kind of exhaustion that came from knowing too much and being able to say too little.

"Elena," he said gently, "we need to be careful."

She finally turned. "Careful? Henrik, the Arctic is changing faster than any model predicts. The vortex is behaving like it's being... guided."

Henrik closed the door. "I know."

Elena blinked. "You know?"

He nodded. "I've been running independent simulations. Off-record. Off-network."

"And?"

Henrik hesitated — a long, heavy pause.

"Elena... the vortex isn't reacting to atmospheric conditions."

She stepped closer. "Then what is it reacting to?"

Henrik swallowed. "Pressure signatures."

"From what?"

He exhaled. "From below."

The room seemed to shrink around them.

"Below the ice?" Elena whispered.
Henrik nodded. "Deep below. Something is creating micro-vibrations — subtle, rhythmic, consistent. They're influencing the upper atmosphere."

Elena felt her pulse quicken. "A natural phenomenon?"

"No," Henrik said. "A natural phenomenon doesn't repeat itself with mathematical precision."

She stared at him. "Then what is it?"

Henrik looked away. "A signal."

The word hung in the air like frost.

Elena turned back to the screen. The vortex pulsed again — a slow, deliberate contraction.

"Someone is doing this," she said.

Henrik didn't argue.

"And the submarine?" she asked.
Henrik's silence was answer enough.

Elena pressed her palm against the cold glass of the window. Outside, the Arctic stretched into infinity — a kingdom of ice hiding secrets older than nations.

“Henrik,” she said softly, “if someone can manipulate the vortex… what else can they manipulate?”

Henrik didn’t answer.

He didn’t need to.

The truth was already in the room.

A soft alarm chimed — not loud, not urgent, but insistent.

Elena turned back to the console.

The vortex had tightened again.

Henrik whispered, “It’s accelerating.”

Elena felt a chill crawl up her spine.

“No,” she said. “It’s responding.”

They stood in silence, watching the Arctic breathe in a way no natural system ever should.

Far away, governments were meeting.
Corporations were plotting.
Economists were warning.

But here, at the top of the world, two scientists were the first to understand the truth:

The Arctic wasn't being observed.
It was being controlled.

And the world had no idea.

"Nature speaks in patterns.
When the pattern changes, something — or someone — is speaking back."
— Dr. Aino Rautio, Finnish Glaciological Philosopher (1975)

CHAPTER VIII — THE SHIFT IN THE CURRENTS

North Atlantic, NATO Oceanic Monitoring Vessel Aquila
03:58 GMT

The ocean was restless.

Not violently — not with the fury of storms — but with a subtle, unnerving tension, like a giant turning beneath the waves. Commander Lucas Hale stood on the bridge of the Aquila, staring at the digital bathymetry map glowing on the main console.

Something was wrong with the currents.

Not wrong in the way sailors feared.
Wrong in the way scientists feared.

Lieutenant Mara Jensen approached, her expression tight. "Sir... the readings are consistent."

Hale didn't look away from the screen. "Run them again."

"We already did. Five times."
He exhaled slowly. "Then tell me what I'm looking at."

Mara hesitated. "A shift in the thermohaline circulation."

Hale turned sharply. "That's impossible."

"I know," she said. "But it's happening."

The thermohaline circulation — the deep-ocean conveyor belt that regulated global climate — did not shift. Not in hours. Not in days. Not in centuries.

Yet here it was, bending like a reed in the wind.

Hale leaned closer to the screen. "What's causing it?"

Mara swallowed. "Pressure anomalies. From the Arctic."

Hale felt a chill crawl up his spine. "The vortex?"

"Indirectly," she said. "The atmospheric contraction is altering surface temperatures. That's cascading into the currents."

Hale stared at her. "That fast?"

"That fast."

He turned back to the map. The currents pulsed in slow, unnatural spirals — the same spirals forming in the sky far to the north.

A pattern.
A rhythm.
A signature.

"Sir," Mara said quietly, "there's something else."
Hale braced himself. "Go on."

She tapped a new display. A sonar trace appeared — faint, masked, gliding beneath the waves like a shadow with purpose.

The same trace Elena had seen.
The same trace Washington had flagged.
The same trace Moscow had denied.

Hale's jaw tightened. "Depth?"
"Three thousand meters."

"Speed?"

"Minimal. Almost stationary."

"Origin?"

Mara shook her head. "Unknown."

Hale stepped back. "So we have a shifting vortex, a shifting current, and a submarine that doesn't belong to anyone."

Mara nodded. "And they're all connected."

The bridge fell silent.
Outside, the North Atlantic rolled under a moonless sky, its surface deceptively calm. But beneath it, the world's circulatory system was being rewritten.

Hale turned to his communications officer. "Send a coded report to Brussels. Priority One."

The officer hesitated. "Sir... what do we tell them?"

Hale looked at the sonar trace — that silent, patient shadow beneath the ice.

"Tell them," he said, "that the Arctic is no longer a region."

He paused.

"It's an actor."

The Aquila continued its slow patrol, unaware that far to the north, the vortex tightened again — a silent pulse echoing through the atmosphere, the ocean, and the fragile balance of the world.

The Arctic was speaking.
And the planet was beginning to listen.

"When the sea changes its rhythm, the wise do not ask why.
They prepare."
— Magnus Eiriksson, Icelandic Oceanographer (1981)

CHAPTER IX — THE MARKET TREMBLE

London, Global Commodities Exchange
09:14 GMT

The trading floor was too loud for a Tuesday morning.

Screens flickered with red and green, traders barked orders into headsets, and the air vibrated with the frantic energy of people who sensed something was wrong but couldn't yet name it.

Amara Singh, senior analyst for Arctic-linked commodities, stood at her glass-walled office overlooking the chaos. She had seen volatility before — oil shocks, currency collapses, political coups — but this felt different.

This felt coordinated.

Her assistant rushed in, breathless. "Amara — you need to see this."

He handed her a tablet.
She scanned the numbers.

Oil futures: +4.7%
Natural gas: +6.1%
Rare earth contracts: +9.3%
Shipping insurance premiums: +12.4%
Arctic freight derivatives: +18.9%

Amara frowned. "This makes no sense. There's no storm. No embargo. No conflict."

Her assistant swallowed. "It's the Arctic data."

Amara froze.

"What data?"

He tapped the screen. A live feed appeared — atmospheric pressure anomalies, vortex contraction metrics, and a new line she hadn't seen before:

THERMOHALINE DEVIATION INDEX: +0.42%

Her pulse quickened. "That's impossible."

"I thought so too," he said. "But NATO confirmed the readings."

Amara stared at the numbers.
A deviation in the thermohaline circulation — even a small one — could alter global shipping patterns, energy flows, and commodity prices.

But this wasn't natural.
It was too fast.
Too precise.

She turned to her assistant. "Who else has this data?"

"Washington. Brussels. Oslo. And..." He hesitated.

"And who?"

"Zurich."

Amara's stomach tightened. Zurich meant private capital. Zurich meant the kind of money that didn't react to markets — it moved them.

She stepped closer to the window. The trading floor below was a storm of motion — traders shouting, screens flashing, algorithms recalibrating.

"Look at them," she said quietly. "They think this is a market event."

Her assistant frowned. "Isn't it?"

Amara shook her head. "No. This is a signal."

He blinked. "A signal of what?"

She turned back to the tablet, her voice steady.

"Someone is manipulating the Arctic. And the markets are responding."

A new alert flashed across the screen:

BREAKING: NORTHERN SEA ROUTE SHIPPING DELAYS EXPECTED — INSURERS RAISE RISK LEVEL

Amara exhaled slowly. "There it is."

"What?"

"The first crack."

She walked to her desk, opened a secure channel, and began typing a message to the Bank of England's crisis unit.

SUBJECT: ARCTIC ANOMALY — ECONOMIC IMPLICATIONS
PRIORITY: IMMEDIATE

Before she could finish, another alert appeared:

UNIDENTIFIED SUBMARINE SIGNATURE DETECTED NEAR GREENLAND RIDGE

Her assistant whispered, "That's the same trace from the Svalbard report."

Amara nodded. "And it's moving south."

The room seemed to tilt around her.
The vortex.
The currents.
The submarine.
The markets.

All threads of the same web.

She closed her eyes for a moment, steadying herself.

"Call the governor," she said. "Tell him the Arctic is no longer a scientific anomaly."

Her assistant hesitated. “Then what is it?”

Amara opened her eyes.

“A geopolitical event.”

She looked down at the trading floor — the shouting, the panic, the screens bleeding red.

“And this,” she added, “is only the beginning.”
Outside, London’s sky was gray and indifferent.
Inside, the world’s financial heart had just felt the first tremor of a storm no one yet understood.

“Markets do not fear chaos.
They fear the moment chaos becomes intentional.”
— Eduardo Salvatierra, Chilean Financial Historian (2008)

CHAPTER X — THE FAULT LINE

Washington, D.C. White House Situation Room
06:12 EST

The Situation Room was colder than usual.

Not in temperature — in mood.
The kind of cold that settles when powerful people realize they are no longer in control.

Director Samuel Harrington sat at the head of the long table, a stack of classified reports in front of him. His jaw was tight, his eyes sharper than usual. Around him sat the National Security Advisor, the Secretary of Defense, the Secretary of Energy, and two senior intelligence chiefs.

The screen behind them displayed a mosaic of data:

the tightening Arctic vortex

the shifting thermohaline currents

the unidentified submarine
the market tremors

the Zurich intelligence intercepts

The room hummed with tension.

The National Security Advisor broke the silence. "We need to determine whether this is a natural event or a coordinated action."

Harrington didn't look up. "It's not natural."

The Secretary of Defense frowned. "You're certain?"

Harrington tapped the folder. "We've seen atmospheric anomalies before. We've seen current deviations. But we've never seen both at the same time, in the same pattern, with the same precision."

The Secretary of Energy leaned forward. "What about the submarine?"

Harrington finally looked up. "It's not Russian. It's not Chinese. It's not ours. And it's not anyone else's."
A heavy silence fell.

The National Security Advisor exhaled. "Then who the hell is it?"

Harrington hesitated — a rare moment of uncertainty.

"We intercepted a communication last night," he said. "Encrypted. Sophisticated. Routed through Zurich."

The Secretary of Defense stiffened. "Zurich? As in—"

"Yes," Harrington said. "Private capital."

The room shifted.
Private capital meant no treaties.
No oversight.

No accountability.

The Secretary of Energy whispered, "A consortium."

Harrington nodded. "A very well-funded one."
The National Security Advisor rubbed his temples. "So we're dealing with a non-state actor capable of manipulating the Arctic?"

"Not manipulating," Harrington corrected. "Influencing."

"And influencing what, exactly?"

Harrington tapped the screen. The vortex pulsed. The currents shifted. The submarine trace glided like a ghost.

"Everything," he said.

The Secretary of Defense leaned back. "We need to consider military options."

Harrington's voice hardened. "No. The Arctic is too fragile. One wrong move and we destabilize the entire region."

The National Security Advisor nodded. "We need intelligence, not force."

The Secretary of Energy added, "And we need to understand their objective."
Harrington closed the folder. "We already do."

The room froze.

He stood, walked to the screen, and pointed at the Arctic map.

"They're not claiming territory," he said. "They're claiming leverage."

The Secretary of Defense frowned. "Leverage over what?"

Harrington turned.

"Over the future."

The room absorbed his words like a blow.

The National Security Advisor whispered, "If they can influence the vortex... the currents... the markets..."

"They can influence nations," Harrington finished.

A long silence followed.

Finally, the Secretary of Defense spoke. "What's our next move?"

Harrington looked at the screen — the vortex tightening like a fist.

"We find them," he said. "Before they decide to show us what else they can do."

Outside, dawn crept over Washington — pale, cold, indifferent.

Inside, the first political fault line had formed.

"The greatest threats are not those we can see.
They are the ones we refuse to name."
— Marcel Duval, French Intelligence Scholar (1992)

CHAPTER XI — THE WARNING IN THE ICE

Reykjavík, Nordic Volcanology & Climate Institute
14:06 GMT

The building trembled.

Not violently — just a subtle vibration, like a giant exhaling beneath the earth. Dr. Freyja Arnadóttir looked up from her workstation, her brow furrowing. The tremor had lasted less than a second, but she felt it in her bones.

Her assistant, Einar, rushed in. "Freyja — you need to see this."

She followed him into the main analysis room, where a cluster of researchers stood around a large screen. The seismic graph was alive with movement — not chaotic, but rhythmic.

Freyja's stomach tightened. "That's not tectonic."

"No," Einar said. "It's too clean."

The graph pulsed again — a perfect wave, evenly spaced, mathematically precise.

Freyja whispered, "It's artificial."

The room fell silent.

She stepped closer, her eyes scanning the data. The pulses were originating from deep beneath the Greenland Ridge — the same region where the unidentified submarine had been detected.

"Cross-reference with oceanic pressure data," she said.

Einar typed rapidly. A second graph appeared — pressure fluctuations in the deep ocean.

The same rhythm.
The same pulse.
The same signature.

Freyja felt a chill crawl up her spine.

"Someone is generating this," she said.

Einar swallowed. "But why?"
Freyja didn't answer. She walked to the window, staring out at the gray Icelandic sky. The wind howled across the harbor, carrying the scent of salt and cold.

Behind her, the seismic graph pulsed again.

Einar spoke softly. "Freyja… what if this is connected to the vortex?"

She closed her eyes.

"It is."

"And the currents?"

"Yes."

"And the submarine?"

She turned. "All of it."

The researchers exchanged uneasy glances.

Freyja returned to the console. "Overlay the atmospheric contraction data."

Einar hesitated. "Are you sure?"

"Do it."

He pressed a key.

The screen filled with three synchronized graphs:

Atmospheric contraction

Deep-ocean pressure pulses

Seismic micro-vibrations

All three aligned perfectly.

A single rhythm.
A single pattern.
A single source.
Freyja whispered, "This isn't a natural system."

Einar stepped back. "Then what is it?"

Freyja stared at the screen, her voice barely audible.

"A message."
The room froze.

"A message from who?" Einar asked.

Freyja shook her head. "Not who. What."

She pointed at the synchronized graphs.

"This is a controlled signal. Someone is using the Arctic like an instrument."

The researchers stared at her, stunned.

Einar whispered, "To communicate?"

"No," Freyja said. "To warn."

The graphs pulsed again — stronger this time.

Freyja felt the tremor beneath her feet.

"Send this to Oslo," she said. "And to Washington. And to Svalbard."

Einar hesitated. "What do we tell them?"

Freyja looked at the screen — the Arctic's heartbeat, steady and unnatural.

"Tell them," she said, "that the ice is speaking."
She paused.

"And we are running out of time to understand what it's saying."

Outside, the Icelandic wind roared across the harbor, carrying with it the first whisper of a truth the world was not ready to face.
"The earth does not tremble without reason.
Sometimes the reason is simply that we refused to listen."
— Dr. Freyja Arnadóttir, Icelandic Seismologist (2024)

CHAPTER XII — THE ARCTIC EQUATION

Brussels, Directorate for Global Economic Stability
07:40 CET

The briefing room was silent.

Not the respectful silence of diplomacy — the heavy, anticipatory silence of people who knew the world had shifted and were about to learn how much.

Dr. Elise Moreau, chief economist of the European Directorate, stood at the head of the table. Her posture was rigid, her expression unreadable. Before her lay a single folder stamped:

CLASSIFIED — LEVEL OMEGA
Prepared by: MARIO LEBRON, M.A. APPLIED ECONOMICS
Subject: Strategic Macroeconomic Assessment of Arctic Resource Dynamics

The delegates — from Germany, France, Spain, Sweden, and the Commission — waited.

Elise opened the folder.

"Ladies and gentlemen," she said, "what you are about to read is the most consequential economic assessment produced in the last twenty years."

She began.

CONFIDENTIAL ECONOMIC DOSSIER
Author: Mario Lebron, M.A. Applied Economics

Title: The Arctic as a Global Balance Sheet
Distribution: Restricted to Directorate-Level Officials

Executive Summary
The Arctic is no longer a peripheral region.
It is a strategic economic fulcrum whose resources, shipping lanes, and climate influence now represent the single largest concentration of untapped global leverage.

Recent anomalies — atmospheric, oceanic, and seismic — indicate that the region is being influenced by an external actor. This actor is not a nation-state.

The implications are profound.

1. Resource Endowment: The Last Great Reserve
A. Energy Reserves
13% of the world's undiscovered oil

30% of undiscovered natural gas

Massive methane hydrate deposits

Economic Implication:
Control of Arctic energy reserves would allow a private actor to influence global energy prices, supply stability, and geopolitical bargaining power.

B. Critical Minerals
The Arctic contains commercially viable concentrations of:

Rare earth elements

Cobalt

Nickel

Titanium

Platinum group metals

Economic Implication:
These minerals are essential for semiconductors, batteries, aerospace, and defense systems.
Control of Arctic minerals = control of 21st-century industrial capacity.

C. Mobility: The Northern Sea Route
Melting ice is opening a corridor that:

Reduces Asia–Europe transit by 40%

Cuts fuel costs by 30–35%

Bypasses chokepoints like Suez and Malacca

Economic Implication:
The Northern Sea Route is a global trade disruptor.
Whoever controls it can influence shipping insurance, freight pricing, and supply chain reliability.
2. The Arctic as a Global Price Stabilizer
The Arctic's resources act as a macro buffer:

Additional energy supply reduces volatility

New shipping lanes reduce transport costs

Rare earth access stabilizes tech production

Diversified supply chains reduce geopolitical risk premiums

Conclusion:
The Arctic is the world's future inflation stabilizer.

If manipulated, it becomes the world's inflation accelerator.

3. Strategic Logic Behind the Current Anomalies
The synchronized anomalies — vortex contraction, thermohaline deviation, deep-ocean pulses — indicate a coordinated influence on Arctic systems.

This influence is:
deliberate

precise

technologically advanced

economically motivated

Assessment:
A private consortium is attempting to reshape Arctic conditions to gain early access to resources and shipping corridors.

This is not sabotage.
This is positioning.

4. Global Economic Risks
A. Market Instability
Early tremors already visible:

Energy futures volatility

Rare earth price spikes
Arctic freight insurance surges

B. Supply Chain Vulnerability
A manipulated Arctic could:

Disrupt semiconductor production

Destabilize battery supply chains

Increase shipping delays

Raise global manufacturing costs

C. Sovereign Wealth Exposure
Nations with Arctic-linked funds (Norway, Canada, Russia) face:

valuation risk

asset repricing

long-term yield instability
5. Strategic Conclusion
"The Arctic is no longer a frontier.

It is a balance sheet — and someone is rewriting the numbers."
— Mario Lebron

A private actor with control over Arctic conditions would possess:

leverage over global energy

leverage over global trade

leverage over global technology

leverage over global inflation

This is not a regional issue.
It is a systemic economic threat.

END OF DOSSIER
Prepared by: Mario Lebron, M.A. Applied Economics
Classification: OMEGA — Do Not Distribute
Elise closed the folder.

The room was silent.
The German delegate finally spoke. "If this is accurate, then the Arctic is the new global reserve."

Elise nodded. "And someone is trying to seize it."

The Spanish representative whispered, "Not a nation... a consortium."

Elise looked at the map on the screen — the vortex tightening like a fist.

"Ladies and gentlemen," she said, "we are not facing a geopolitical crisis."

She paused.

"We are facing an economic coup."

Outside, Brussels continued its morning routine — unaware that the world's financial architecture had just been exposed as fragile.
Inside, the truth settled like ice.

"Economics is the quiet architect of power.
The Arctic is its newest blueprint."
— Håkon Sturluson, Icelandic Economic Historian (2011)

CHAPTER XIII — THE SILENT WATCHERS

Barents Sea, NATO Forward Surveillance Zone
02:11 GMT

The sea was black.

Not the blue-black of deep water, but the metallic black of a world without moonlight — a world where machines, not stars, ruled the night.

Commander Sofia Ristović stood in the control room of the HMS Vigilant, one of NATO's most advanced nuclear-powered submarines. The hum of the reactor was steady, almost soothing, but the tension in the room was anything but.

"Status," she said.

Her sonar officer, Lieutenant Harris, didn't look up from his console. "Still nothing identifiable, ma'am. But the distortion is persistent."

Sofia narrowed her eyes. "Show me."

Harris tapped a key. The sonar display shifted — a field of blue punctuated by faint, irregular ripples. Not noise. Not interference.

A presence.

Sofia leaned closer. "That's not geological."

"No, ma'am."

"And it's not biological."

"Definitely not."

Sofia exhaled slowly. "Then it's engineered."

The room fell silent.

The Vigilant had been tracking the unidentified submarine signature for days — a ghost beneath the ice, moving with unnatural precision. But now, something else was happening.

The ghost was no longer hiding.
It was watching.

Above the Ice — Patrol Drone 'Aquila-9'
Altitude: 42,000 ft

The drone cut through the Arctic night like a blade of silver. Its sensors scanned the ice below — thermal, infrared, synthetic aperture radar, magnetometric imaging.

Nothing escaped it.

But tonight, something challenged it.

"Control, this is Aquila-9," the drone operator said from the NATO command center in Tromsø. "We're picking up a radar anomaly."

The supervisor frowned. "Define anomaly."

“Something is bending our signal.”

The room stiffened.

“Is it jamming?”

“No. It’s… redirecting.”

The supervisor leaned in. “Redirecting how?”

The operator swallowed. “Like it’s studying us.”

A chill swept through the command center.

On the Ice — Svalbard Radar Array ‘FROST-3’
22:19 UTC

Dr. Elena Markov stood in front of the massive radar display, her heart pounding. The array was one of the most sophisticated in the world — capable of tracking micro-movements beneath the ice sheet.

Tonight, it was overwhelmed.

“Look at this,” she said.

The radar technician zoomed in. A cluster of signals pulsed beneath the ice — rhythmic, coordinated, intelligent.

Elena whispered, “It’s mapping us.”

The technician looked at her. “Mapping what?”

“Everything,” she said. “Submarines. Drones. Satellites. Our entire surveillance network.”

The technician swallowed. “But who has that capability?”

Elena didn’t answer.

She already knew.

Back Beneath the Sea — HMS Vigilant
Lieutenant Harris stiffened. “Ma’am — new contact!”

Sofia turned sharply. “Where?”

“Directly beneath us.”
The room froze.

Sofia stepped forward. “Depth?”

“Four thousand meters.”
“Distance?”

Harris swallowed. “Two hundred meters.”

Sofia’s blood ran cold.

The ghost submarine — the one no nation claimed — had risen directly beneath the Vigilant.

Not attacking.

Not fleeing.
Just... observing.

"Ma'am," Harris whispered, "it's pinging us."

Sofia's eyes widened. "Active sonar?"

"No. Something else. Something... coded."

The submarine was sending a signal.

A message.

Sofia steadied herself. "Record everything. Do not respond."

The Vigilant drifted in the black water, silent and still, while the unknown submarine pulsed its strange, rhythmic signal — the same rhythm detected in the vortex, the currents, the seismic pulses.

A single intelligence.
A single design.
A single hand.

Sofia whispered, "What are you?"

The ghost submarine sank back into the abyss, disappearing as silently as it had arrived.

The Vigilant's crew exhaled as one.
But Sofia didn't.

She knew what this meant.

The Arctic was no longer a battlefield.
It was a sensor field — and someone else had already mastered it.

“The most dangerous weapon is not the one that fires.
It is the one that sees everything.”
— Admiral Viktor Lobanov, Russian Naval Strategist (2003)

CHAPTER XIV — THE EDGE OF THE STORM

Oslo, Joint Arctic Security Council Emergency Session
11:22 CET

The chamber was built for diplomacy, not crisis.
Tall windows. Soft lighting. A circular table meant to symbolize cooperation.
But today, the room felt like a bunker — sealed, tense, suffocating.

Representatives from Norway, the United States, Canada, Denmark, Iceland, and the EU sat in rigid silence as the screens flickered to life.

At the center of the table stood Ingrid Solberg, Norway's Minister of Arctic Affairs. Her voice was steady, but her eyes betrayed the weight of what she was about to reveal.

"Ladies and gentlemen," she began, "the Arctic is no longer stable."

She tapped a control panel.

The first screen displayed the tightening vortex.
The second showed the thermohaline deviation.
The third showed the seismic pulses.
The fourth showed the ghost submarine.
The fifth displayed the economic dossier by Mario Lebron, M.A. Applied Economics.

The room shifted.

Ingrid continued, "We now have confirmation that these events are not isolated. They are synchronized."

The Canadian representative leaned forward. "Synchronized by what?"

Ingrid hesitated — a rare moment of fear.

"By someone," she said.

A murmur rippled through the chamber.

The U.S. representative, a stern man with a voice like gravel, spoke next. "We've tracked the unidentified submarine. It's not Russian. It's not Chinese. It's not ours. It's not anyone's."
The Danish delegate whispered, "Then whose is it?"

The American didn't blink. "A private actor."

Silence.

Ingrid tapped the table again. A new image appeared — a map of the Arctic with glowing points marking anomalies.

"These," she said, "are the locations where the anomalies intersect."

The Icelandic representative frowned. "Intersect? How?"

Ingrid turned to the screen. "Atmospheric pressure. Oceanic currents. Seismic pulses. Radar distortions. Submarine movement."

She paused.

"All following the same rhythm."

The room froze.
The EU delegate whispered, "A coordinated pattern..."

Ingrid nodded. "Yes. And according to the economic analysis provided by Mr. Lebron, this pattern aligns with strategic resource zones, shipping corridors, and mineral fields."

The Canadian representative exhaled. "So this isn't sabotage."

"No," Ingrid said. "It's preparation."

The American leaned forward. "For what?"

Ingrid looked at the screen — at the vortex tightening like a fist.

"For control."

The room erupted.

Voices clashed — accusations, fears, demands.
The chamber meant for diplomacy became a storm of panic.

Ingrid raised her voice. "Enough!"
The room fell silent.

She continued, "We are facing a non-state actor with capabilities beyond any known private entity. They are manipulating the Arctic environment to gain strategic, economic, and geopolitical leverage."

The Danish delegate whispered, "This is an economic coup."

Ingrid nodded. "Yes. And we are already behind."

The American representative clenched his jaw. "What do you propose?"

Ingrid looked at the screen — at the ghost submarine, the vortex, the currents, the seismic pulses.

"We need to coordinate intelligence.
We need to share data.
We need to unify our response."

She paused.

"And we need to find them before they decide to escalate."

The room fell into a heavy, suffocating silence.

Outside, snow drifted gently over Oslo — calm, quiet, indifferent.

Inside, the world's Arctic powers realized they were no longer dealing with a mystery.

They were dealing with an adversary.

And the storm was only beginning.

"The greatest danger is not the enemy we see.
It is the one who learns to move without being seen."
— Ingrid Solberg, Arctic Security Address (1978)

CHAPTER XV — THE FRACTURE IN THE SHADOWS

Zurich, Helix International Holdings, Sublevel 3
23:41 CET

The room was colder than the rest of the building.

Not by accident — by design.
Cold sharpened the mind.
Cold kept people honest.

Dr. Adrian Keller stepped into the subterranean chamber, where the true leadership of the consortium gathered. The obsidian table was smaller here, the lighting dimmer, the atmosphere heavier.

Tonight, the air felt different.
Tense.
Charged.

The silver-haired woman — the one whose voice could silence a room with a single syllable — sat at the head of the table. Her expression was unreadable.

"You're late," she said.

Adrian bowed his head slightly. "I was reviewing the latest intercepts."

"And?"

Adrian placed a tablet on the table. The hologram flickered to life — atmospheric contraction data, thermohaline deviations, seismic pulses, radar distortions, and the ghost submarine's latest movements.

But this time, something new appeared.

A dossier.

CLASSIFIED — LEVEL OMEGA
Prepared by: MARIO LEBRON, M.A. APPLIED ECONOMICS
Subject: Strategic Macroeconomic Assessment of Arctic Resource Dynamics

The room stiffened.

The man in the charcoal suit leaned forward. "They have the full picture."

Adrian nodded. "Yes. And they understand the economic implications."

The silver-haired woman's eyes narrowed. "How accurate is his analysis?"

Adrian hesitated — a dangerous act in this room.

"Very accurate," he said. "Too accurate."

A murmur rippled through the chamber.

The woman tapped the table. "Show me."

Adrian swiped. The hologram displayed the key sections of your analysis — the resource triad, the inflation buffer, the shipping corridor leverage, the mineral dominance, the systemic risk.

The consortium members watched in silence.

When the hologram faded, the woman spoke.

"So the world finally understands the value of what we are taking."

Adrian swallowed. "They also understand the danger."

The man in charcoal suit frowned. "Danger to whom?"

"To us," Adrian said. "The Arctic Council is mobilizing. NATO is coordinating. The markets are reacting. The scientists are connecting the anomalies."

The woman's voice was soft, but lethal. "And the submarine?"

Adrian exhaled. "It revealed itself."

The room froze.

"Explain," she said.

Adrian tapped the screen. A sonar trace appeared — the moment the ghost submarine rose beneath the HMS Vigilant, sending its coded pulse.

"It approached a NATO nuclear submarine," Adrian said. "Deliberately. It sent a signal."

The woman's eyes sharpened. "A warning?"

"No," Adrian said. "A demonstration."

The room fell into a heavy silence.

Finally, the man in charcoal suit spoke. "We need to accelerate Phase Two."

Adrian shook his head. "Phase Two will expose us."

The man glared. "We are already exposed."

Adrian stepped forward. "No. Not yet. But if we escalate now, they will trace the anomalies back to us. They will connect the submarine. They will understand the technology."

The woman raised a hand. Silence returned instantly.

"Adrian," she said, "what do you propose?"

Adrian hesitated — the entire room watching him.

"We slow down," he said. "We let the world panic. We let them argue. We let them fracture. Fear will do more for us than force."

The man in charcoal suit scoffed. "Cowardice."

Adrian turned to him. "Strategy."

The woman studied Adrian for a long moment.

Then she spoke.

"Phase Two is postponed."

The man in charcoal suit slammed his fist on the table. "You're making a mistake."

The woman didn't look at him. "No. I'm preventing one."

Adrian exhaled quietly.

But the man in charcoal suit wasn't finished.

He leaned forward, his voice low and venomous. "If we wait too long, the world will unite. And then we lose everything."

The woman finally turned to him.

"Then perhaps," she said, "you should remember that impatience is the enemy of power."

The room fell silent.

The meeting ended.

But as Adrian walked toward the elevator, he felt something he had never felt before inside the consortium:

A fracture.

A crack in the unity.
A split in the vision.
A shadow within the shadows.

The Arctic was shifting.
The world was awakening.
And now, even the consortium was beginning to fear what they had unleashed.

"Power does not crumble from the outside.
It fractures from within."
— Elena Varga, Political Philosopher (2014)

CHAPTER XVI — THE NEW POWERS OF THE ATLANTIC

North Atlantic Treaty Headquarters. Brussels
18:03 CET

The conference hall was built for ceremony — flags, marble, polished wood — but tonight it felt like a war room. Delegates from twenty-nine nations sat in rigid silence as the screens flickered to life.

Admiral Jonathan Pierce, Supreme Allied Commander Atlantic, stood at the podium. His uniform was immaculate, but his eyes betrayed the truth:

He had not slept.

"Ladies and gentlemen," he began, "the Atlantic is no longer stable."

He tapped a control panel.

The first screen displayed the shifting thermohaline currents.
The second showed the Arctic vortex tightening.
The third showed the seismic pulses.
The fourth showed the ghost submarine.
The fifth displayed the radar distortions from Svalbard.
The sixth showed the economic dossier by Mario Lebron, M.A. Applied Economics.

A murmur rippled through the room.

Pierce continued, his voice steady but heavy.

"For the first time in modern history, the Atlantic's strategic balance is being influenced by a non-state actor."

The German representative leaned forward. "Influenced how?"

Pierce turned to the screen.

"By controlling the Arctic."

The room froze.

He continued, "We have confirmed that the anomalies — atmospheric, oceanic, seismic, and electromagnetic — are synchronized. They follow a pattern. A rhythm. A design."

The French delegate whispered, "A design implies intent."

Pierce nodded. "It does."

He tapped the screen again.

A new image appeared — a map of the North Atlantic with glowing lines tracing the altered currents.

"These shifts," Pierce said, "are already affecting naval mobility, sonar propagation, and satellite communication. Our submarines are losing stealth. Our drones are losing clarity. Our radars are losing reliability."

The Canadian representative stiffened. "This is environmental warfare."

“No,” Pierce said. “This is environmental leverage.”

He stepped away from the podium.

“Ladies and gentlemen, the Atlantic has always been the backbone of Western power. Trade. Energy. Security. Intelligence. Mobility.”
He paused.

“And now, someone is rewriting that backbone.”

The room fell silent.

Pierce continued, “We have identified three immediate threats.”

1. Strategic Mobility Disruption
The altered currents are:

slowing naval transit

distorting sonar

creating blind zones

weakening anti-submarine nets

“Our fleets are no longer invisible,” Pierce said. “But theirs is.”

2. Economic Leverage
He gestured toward your dossier.

"According to Mr. Lebron's analysis, the Arctic is the world's new balance sheet. Whoever controls it controls energy, minerals, shipping, and inflation."

He paused.

"And someone is trying to control it."

3. Technological Superiority
Pierce tapped the screen again.

A new image appeared — the ghost submarine rising beneath the HMS Vigilant.

"This vessel," he said, "is beyond any known military capability. It is silent. It is precise. It is intelligent. And it is not alone."

The room erupted.

Voices clashed — fear, anger, disbelief.

Pierce raised his voice. "Enough!"

Silence returned.
He continued, "We are witnessing the emergence of a new power — not a nation, not an alliance, but a private entity with the resources of a state and the ambition of an empire."

The Norwegian representative whispered, "A shadow empire."

Pierce nodded. "Yes. And they are using the Arctic as their throne."

He stepped back from the podium.

"Ladies and gentlemen, the Atlantic is no longer ours. Not fully. Not safely. Not predictably."

He paused.

"We must adapt. We must coordinate. We must prepare."

His voice hardened.

"Because the next phase will not be subtle."

The room fell into a heavy, suffocating silence.

Outside, the Atlantic winds battered the coast — restless, shifting, uncertain.

Inside, the leaders of the Western world realized they were no longer the only powers in the ocean.

A new force had risen.
Silent.
Invisible.
Unbound by borders.
And the Atlantic, once the heart of global stability, was becoming the stage for a new kind of empire.

“Empires are not born from land or flags.
They are born from the ability to shape the world without being seen.”
— Admiral Jonathan Pierce, Atlantic Address (2006)

CHAPTER XVII — THE COUNTERMEASURE

Svalbard Global Observatory, Command Annex
00:14 UTC

The storm outside was relentless.

Wind hammered the steel walls, snow whipped across the windows in violent spirals, and the Arctic night pressed against the building like a living thing. Inside, the command annex buzzed with a different kind of storm — one made of urgency, fear, and the first sparks of defiance.

Dr. Elena Markov stood at the center of the room, surrounded by screens displaying the synchronized anomalies: the vortex pulse, the thermohaline deviation, the seismic rhythm, the radar distortions, the ghost submarine's last known position.

She had not slept in thirty hours.

Henrik Dahl entered, his face pale, his breath visible in the cold air. "Elena... they're ready."

She nodded. "Bring them in."

The door opened.

Three figures stepped inside:

Admiral Jonathan Pierce, Supreme Allied Commander Atlantic

Ingrid Solberg, Norway's Minister of Arctic Affairs

Dr. Elise Moreau, chief economist of the European Directorate

The room shifted.
This was no longer a scientific meeting.

This was a war council.

Elena gestured to the main screen. "Thank you for coming. We don't have much time."

Pierce crossed his arms. "We read your latest report. The pulses are accelerating."

Elena nodded. "Yes. And the pattern is changing."
Ingrid frowned. "Changing how?"

Elena tapped the console. The seismic graph expanded — the rhythmic pulses now forming a new shape.

A wave.
A rising wave.

Henrik whispered, "It's building toward something."

Pierce stepped closer. "A detonation?"

"No," Elena said. "A release."

The room froze.

Elise Moreau spoke softly. "A release of what?"

Elena turned to her. “Pressure. Heat. Energy. The Arctic is being primed like a system under tension.”

Pierce’s jaw tightened. “A trigger.”
Elena nodded. “Yes. And we believe the consortium is preparing to activate it.”

Ingrid exhaled. “Phase Two.”

Elena looked at her. “You know about Phase Two?”

Ingrid nodded grimly. “We intercepted fragments. Nothing complete. But enough to know it’s the escalation.”

Pierce stepped forward. “We need a countermeasure.”

Elena hesitated. “We’ve been working on one.”

Henrik brought up a new display — a complex model of the Arctic’s atmospheric and oceanic systems.

Elena continued, “If we can disrupt the rhythm — even slightly — we may be able to break the synchronization.”

Pierce frowned. “You want to interfere with the pattern?”

“Yes.”
“That’s dangerous.”

Elena met his gaze. “So is doing nothing.”

The room fell silent.

Elise Moreau stepped forward. "What do you need?"

Elena took a breath. "Three things."

She raised a finger.

"First: full access to NATO's deep-ocean sensor grid."

Pierce nodded slowly. "Granted."

A second finger.

"Second: real-time satellite telemetry from the EU's polar orbiters."

Elise nodded. "Done."
A third finger.

"And third: Norway's experimental atmospheric modulator."

Ingrid stiffened. "Elena… that device is untested."

"I know."

"It could destabilize the vortex."

"I know."

"It could make everything worse."

Elena's voice hardened. "And if we do nothing, the consortium will make everything worse."

The room absorbed her words like a blow.

Finally, Admiral Pierce spoke.

"What's the objective?"
Elena turned to the screen — the rising wave of pulses.

"To break the pattern," she said. "To disrupt the signal. To force the Arctic back into a natural state."

Pierce nodded. "And if it works?"

Elena exhaled. "We buy time."

"And if it fails?"

Elena looked at him.

"Then the Arctic becomes theirs."

The room fell into a heavy, suffocating silence.

Ingrid finally spoke. "When do we begin?"

Elena turned to the window — the storm raging outside, the Arctic trembling beneath it.

"Now," she said. "Before they trigger Phase Two."

"When the world stands at the edge of the storm, the first act of courage is simply to push back."
— Dr. Elena Markov, Svalbard Address (1976)

CHAPTER XVIII — THE FIRST INTERFERENCE

Norwegian Sea, NATO Hydrophone Relay Vessel Aegir
04:52 UTC — January 2026

The sea was unnaturally calm.

Not peaceful — calm in the way a held breath is calm, in the way a predator is calm before it strikes. The Aegir drifted through the gray dawn, its deck slick with frost, its antennas angled toward the sky like spears.

Below deck, the operations room glowed with dim red light. Analog dials, oscilloscopes, and hydrophone monitors lined the walls. The air smelled of oil, metal, and tension.

Admiral Jonathan Pierce stood at the center, coat unbuttoned, jaw tight.

"Status," he said.

The communications officer adjusted a dial. "NATO hydrophone grid is online. All Atlantic nodes reporting."

Pierce nodded. "And Svalbard?"
"Standing by. Dr. Markov is ready."

Pierce exhaled. "Patch her through."

A burst of static filled the room, then Elena's voice emerged — strained, focused, unshakable.

"Admiral, we're detecting the pulse rising again. The next wave will peak in six minutes."

Pierce glanced at the clock. "Understood. We're ready."

Henrik's voice joined hers. "Remember — the interference must be synchronized within a two-second window. If we miss it—"

"We won't," Pierce said.

The line crackled. "God help us if we do."

Svalbard — Atmospheric Resonator Station
04:53 UTC

The resonator tower loomed over the icy ridge like a skeletal giant — a Cold War experiment never meant to be activated outside a laboratory.

Tonight, it was humanity's only hope.

Elena stood at the control panel, fingers trembling over the analog switches. The machine hummed with a low, unsettling frequency.

Ingrid Solberg entered, breathless. "Elena — the next pulse is forming."

Elena nodded. "I can feel it."

Ingrid hesitated. "Are you sure this will work?"

Elena didn't look up. "No."

A beat.

"But I'm sure we have no choice."

North Atlantic — Subsurface
04:54 UTC

Deep beneath the waves, the ghost submarine drifted in the abyss — silent, patient, watching.

Its hull reflected no sonar.
Its engines emitted no detectable signature.
Its presence was known only through the distortions it left behind.

Tonight, it was moving.

Slowly.
Deliberately.
Toward the Aegir.

Aboard the Aegir
04:55 UTC

The hydrophone monitors began to tremble.

The pulse was rising — a deep, rhythmic vibration that resonated through the hull, through the instruments, through the bones of every man aboard.

The sonar officer stiffened. "Admiral… the anomaly is approaching."

Pierce turned sharply. "Distance?"

"Three kilometers."

"Depth?"

"Unknown."

Pierce clenched his jaw. "It's watching us."

The pulse grew stronger.

Elena's voice crackled through the radio. "Admiral — prepare to transmit the counter-signal."

Pierce nodded to his crew. "Begin the sequence."
The technicians activated the interference array — a series of underwater transmitters designed to disrupt the synchronized Arctic rhythm.

The dials spun.
The lights flickered.
The ship vibrated.

"Ready," the officer said.

Pierce gripped the console. "On my mark."

Svalbard — Resonator Tower
04:56 UTC

Elena watched the seismic graph spike.

“It’s coming,” she whispered.

Henrik adjusted the frequency modulators. “We’re aligned with the Aegir.”

Elena placed her hand on the activation lever.
“Three minutes,” she said.

Ingrid swallowed. “And if the resonator overloads?”

Elena didn’t answer.

The Pulse
04:57 UTC

The Arctic trembled.

The vortex tightened.
The currents shifted.
The seismic rhythm surged.

The ghost submarine accelerated.

The world held its breath.

Aboard the Aegir
04:58 UTC

Pierce raised his hand.

“Stand by...”

The pulse hit the hydrophones like a physical blow — the monitors spiking, the lights flickering, the hull groaning.

“NOW!” Pierce shouted.

The interference array activated.

A deep, resonant counter-signal surged into the ocean — a wave of sound engineered to disrupt the Arctic’s unnatural rhythm.

The room shook.
The instruments screamed.
The crew staggered.

“Signal holding!” the officer shouted.

Pierce gritted his teeth. “Maintain it!”

Svalbard — Resonator Tower
04:59 UTC

Elena pulled the lever.

The resonator roared to life — a towering beam of atmospheric vibration that shot into the sky, bending the air, distorting the clouds, shaking the ice.

The storm above twisted violently.

Henrik shouted over the noise. “We’re destabilizing the pattern!”

Elena’s eyes widened. “It’s working!”

The Arctic
05:00 UTC

For the first time, the rhythm faltered.

The pulse stuttered.
The vortex wavered.
The currents hesitated.

The ghost submarine stopped.

Then—

It turned.

And fled.

Aboard the Aegir
05:01 UTC

The interference array powered down.

Silence.

The sonar officer stared at his screen. "Admiral… the anomaly is retreating."

Pierce exhaled — the first breath he'd taken in minutes.

"We did it," he whispered.

But the officer wasn't smiling.

"Sir… before it left… it transmitted something."

Pierce turned slowly. "What kind of transmission?"

The officer swallowed.

"A countdown."

"Victory is not the moment the enemy retreats.
It is the moment you realize why they did."
— Aurelio Santamar, Reflections on Endurance (1974)

CHAPTER XIX — THE COUNTDOWN BEGINS (Present Day)

Zurich, Helix International Holdings, Sublevel 3
06:12 CET — Present Day

The room felt colder than usual.
Not physically — psychologically.
The kind of cold that settles when powerful people realize the world has begun to understand their game.

Dr. Adrian Keller stepped into the subterranean chamber, the hum of servers echoing through the dimly lit space. The obsidian table reflected the glow of encrypted holographic displays. The consortium's core leadership was already assembled.

The silver-haired woman sat at the head of the table, posture perfect, expression unreadable.
The man in the charcoal suit stood behind her, hands clasped, eyes sharp with restrained fury.

"You're late," the woman said.

Adrian swallowed. "I came as soon as I saw the alert."

The man in charcoal suit stepped forward. "Then you know."

Adrian nodded. "The interference."

The woman tapped the table. A hologram flickered to life — seismic pulses, atmospheric distortions, oceanic anomalies, and the ghost submarine's telemetry.

All disrupted.
All fractured.
All temporarily broken.

"They hit the pattern," Adrian said. "Hard."

The man in charcoal suit slammed his fist on the table. "They shouldn't have been able to."

Adrian didn't flinch. "They shouldn't have known what to target."

The woman's eyes narrowed. "But they did."

Adrian placed a digital folder on the table. "Because someone on the outside understands the economic logic behind our operation."

The hologram shifted to a classified document.

STRATEGIC MACROECONOMIC ASSESSMENT OF ARCTIC RESOURCE DYNAMICS
Prepared by: MARIO LEBRON, M.A. Applied Economics

The woman read the first lines.

Her expression changed.

Recognition.
Respect.
Concern.

"This analysis is… sophisticated," she said.

Adrian nodded. "It identifies the Arctic as a global balance sheet. It outlines the leverage points. It predicts our objectives."

The man in charcoal suit growled, "Then eliminate him."

The woman raised a hand. "No."

Silence.

She continued, "Killing him confirms his importance. Instead, we watch him. We learn from him. And we stay ahead."

Adrian exhaled quietly.

The woman tapped the table again. "Now… the countdown."

The man in charcoal suit placed a small cylindrical device on the table — matte black, pulsing with a slow red light.

Adrian stiffened. "You activated it?"

The man smiled coldly. "Of course."

The woman's voice cut through the room. "Adrian. What does the countdown mean?"

Adrian swallowed. "It means Phase Two is unavoidable."

"And Phase Two is…?"

Adrian hesitated.

“Destabilization.”

The woman nodded. “Correct.”

The man in charcoal suit leaned forward. “They pushed back. Now we escalate.”

Adrian’s voice trembled. “If we escalate now, they’ll trace the anomalies. They’ll identify the submarine. They’ll—”

The woman interrupted him.

“They’ll be too late.”

She tapped the device.

The red light pulsed faster.

Adrian felt his stomach drop. “How long?”

The man in charcoal suit smiled.

“Seventy-two hours.”

Adrian’s breath caught. “That’s not enough time for them to—”

“It’s enough,” the woman said.

She stood, her silhouette framed by the cold glow of the holograms.

"Ladies and gentlemen," she said, "the countdown has begun."

She turned toward the elevator.

"And when it ends… the Arctic will belong to us."

The doors closed behind her.
Adrian stared at the pulsing red light.

Seventy-two hours.
Three days.
After that, the world would change forever.

"The most dangerous moment is not when the enemy strikes.
It is when they decide the time has come."
— Elena Varga, Strategic Reflections (2022)

EPILOGUE — THE SILENCE AFTER THE SIGNAL

Somewhere Above the Arctic Circle
Present Day

The storm had passed.

Not ended — passed.
The kind of storm that leaves the world changed, even if the sky pretends otherwise.

A thin band of pale sunlight cut across the horizon, illuminating the fractured ice fields below. The Arctic looked peaceful, almost innocent, as if the last seventy-two hours had been nothing more than a bad dream.

But the people who knew the truth understood:

The Arctic was never innocent.
And it was no longer silent.

A lone research aircraft — NATO designation Aurora-7 — drifted through the calm air, its engines humming softly. Inside, Dr. Elena Markov sat alone, staring at the data streaming across her tablet.
The countermeasure had worked.
The pattern had broken.
The consortium had retreated.

For now.

She zoomed in on the last seismic reading.
A faint pulse.

Barely detectable.
But unmistakable.

The rhythm had changed — not vanished.

Her breath caught.

“They’re adapting,” she whispered.

The cockpit door opened. Admiral Jonathan Pierce stepped inside, his face lined with exhaustion.

“Elena,” he said quietly. “We need to talk.”

She turned the tablet toward him. “Look.”

He studied the pulse. His jaw tightened.

“That’s not the old pattern.”

“No,” Elena said. “It’s a new one.”

Pierce exhaled. “So the countdown wasn’t the end.”

Elena shook her head. “It was the beginning.”

The aircraft banked gently, revealing the vast expanse of ice below — a white desert stretching to infinity.

Pierce looked out the window. “We bought time.”

Elena nodded. “But not peace.”

He turned to her. "What do you think they'll do next?"

Elena stared at the pulse on her screen — steady, patient, evolving.

"They'll wait," she said. "They'll watch. They'll learn from our interference."

"And then?"

Elena closed her eyes.

"They'll try again."

Pierce stood in silence for a long moment.

Then he said, "We'll be ready."

Elena opened her eyes. "Will we?"

Pierce didn't answer.

Because they both knew the truth:

The consortium had resources beyond nations.
Technology beyond militaries.
Patience beyond politics.

And now, they had a reason to strike harder.

The aircraft continued north, slicing through the cold air like a blade. Below, the ice shifted — subtle, almost imperceptible.

A tremor.
A whisper.
A promise.

The Arctic was speaking again.
And somewhere, in a room of glass and steel, a woman with silver hair watched the same pulse on her own screen.

She smiled.

"Phase Three," she said softly. "Soon."

"The end of a storm is not peace.
It is the moment the world decides whether to rebuild... or prepare for the next one."
— Mario A. Lebron, Reflections on the Arctic Crisis (2026)

FINAL AUTHOR'S NOTE

There are stories we write because they entertain, and there are stories we write because they warn.
This book belongs to the second category.

The Arctic, in all its silence and indifference, has always been a mirror. It reflects not only the fragility of our climate, but the fragility of our assumptions — about power, about stability, about the permanence of the systems we take for granted. What you have read is fiction, yes, but it is fiction arranged around truths that are neither speculative nor distant.

The world does not need villains to collapse.
It only needs incentives.

Every empire, every corporation, every consortium, every government — they all respond to the same gravitational pull: resources, leverage, and the illusion of control. The Arctic simply magnifies these impulses. It is the last frontier where ambition can still hide behind ice and silence.

If this book has a message, it is this:

Power does not always announce itself. Sometimes it whispers beneath the ice.

The technologies described here, the economic vulnerabilities, the geopolitical tensions — they are not fantasies. They are extrapolations of trends already visible to anyone willing to look past the headlines and into the data. The Arctic is changing. The incentives are changing with it. And history has shown, time and again, that when the environment shifts, so does the architecture of power.

I encourage every reader to conduct their own independent research.
Do not take my word for anything.
Interrogate the facts.
Follow the incentives.
Look at the maps.
Look at the markets.
Look at the silence.

Fiction is merely the lens.
Reality is the landscape.

Thank you for walking through it with me.

REFERENCES & CITATIONS

A Curated Reference List for Further Study and Verification

Bellancini, Vittorio S. Stability and the Modern State: Essays in Applied Macroeconomics. Rome: Istituto di Analisi Economica, 1995.

Brenner, Robert. "Energy Markets and Structural Adjustment in the 21st Century." Journal of Global Economics 18, no. 4 (2019): 221–247.

Cárdenas, Luis A. Hemispheric Integration and the Future of Energy Security. Buenos Aires: Fundación del Sur, 2021.

González, Marta E. "Institutional Continuity and Long-Term Development." Latin American Policy Review 12, no. 2 (2020): 45–63.

International Maritime Institute. Atlantic Corridors and the Future of Global Trade. Rotterdam: IMI Press, 2024.

Markov, Elena. "Polar Oscillation Irregularities and Arctic Systemic Stress." Nordic Geophysical Letters 44, no. 1 (2025): 3–29.

Mori, Jianyu. Systems of Continuity: Essays on Stability and Civilization. Osaka: Horizon Press, 1968.

Nishida, Haruto. "Foundations of Enduring Growth." Kyoto Economic Letters 7, no. 1 (1911): 3–14.

Shumenstein, Edmund. "The Responsibility of Surplus Nations." Lecture delivered at Tel Aviv University, Department of Macroeconomics, 1985.

Solberg, Ingrid. Arctic Governance and the New Strategic Frontier. Oslo: Nordic Policy Institute, 2023.

Liang, Wen-Shu. Destiny and the Architecture of Nations. Qingdao: Eastern Meridian Publishing, 1924.

World Energy Forum. Global Energy Outlook 2025. Geneva: WEF Publications, 2025.

Books by Milton Rothbard
Geopolitical & Historical Thrillers

- The Antarctic Covenant
- The Energy Reckoning
- The Geography of Power
- The Lithium Pact
- The Lithium Triangle
- The Pact of Steel & Salt
- Pacts of Survival
- Quantum Archipelago
- The Arctic Vortex
- The Hormuz Economy

Espionage & Political Noir

- Café Buenos Aires
- The Maestro of Minds
- The Severian Manuscript
- The Parallel Shadow
- The Last Luthier
- Agent Harrison
- Project Copenhagen

Women's Romance

- The Velvet Invitation
- Giovanna's Poetry
- Curves Beneath Portofino
- Romance & Steel in Andalucia
- The Bookshop on Rue The Rivoli

Historical & Mythic Fiction

- Aurelia of Rome
- Bushido Masters
- The Andalusian Courtship
- The Chronicles of the Iron Crusade
- Viri Templari
- The Untold Story of Ypres

Crime, Mystery, Drama & Suspense

- The Watchmaker of Geneva
- The Vicarious
- My Girl of Bensonhurst (Blood in the Rain / Clan Wars)
- The Concierge

Comedy General & Corporate Comedy

- The Fool's Menu
- The Last Honest Economist
- Les Imbeciles

www.ingramcontent.com/pod-product-compliance
Lightning Source LLC
LaVergne TN
LVHW022006200926
848481LV00007B/2260
* 9 7 9 8 9 5 1 1 5 3 3 4 0 *